If beauty in life
Cannot be viewed
From where you stand
Learn to bend.

XO

— neow

In the Dance

In the Dance

Illustrated by
Yoko Asari

Poetry by
Ray Blanchard

Published by

The Quantum Company©
P.O. Box 10281
Portland, Oregon 97210

Design: EGRET PRESS DESIGN SERVICES
Jacelen Pete and Larry Miller

ISBN 0-9641382-0-4

To my son

Harmony

The peaceful man has a quiet heart

He is happy in simple ways

And does not worry

He touches the earth

He embraces the sky

Vision

Everything in the world
Begins as a vision
A clear view
Is the source of creation

Birth

One always adores

The newborn child

Glowing

With the presence of God

Youth

The young spirit is precious

There is so much to know

To be free forever

It needs space to grow

Renewal

Be gentle with yourself

Rest

Fill up the empty places

And be strong again

The Great Mystery of Being

The young and the old search for truth

But it is elusive

It cannot be found

It comes from experience

Yielding

Learn to be like the water

Powerful

Life force on earth

Soft and yielding

Nothing stands in its way

Following the Heart

Stay with your ideals

Go forth

Follow your heart

Dreams are waiting for you

Love

Love each other tenderly

The way you love yourself

To love is oneness

Natural Knowing

Return to the innocent state
A pure mind knowing naturally
What the clever one learns in a lifetime

Appearances

Don't be misled

The surface of things is only for show

Look deeper to the essence

On Misfortune

When you have misfortune

Do not lose your faith

Keep a good heart

Make your skin tough

And continue on your way

Dreams

The loftiest dreams are started

From a handful of clay

Build many sandcastles

And have a kingdom in the sky

Joy

When joy is in your heart

The spirit dances free

Happy with yourself

And what you want to be

Self Mastery

As you strive

Remember the ways of the master

Keep your head up in the clouds

And the Earth as your center

Wealth

Take care to nurture the one you love
With the good and simple things
The one who has this kind of love
Is rich beyond his dreams

Struggle

Human beings often struggle for existence

But if you are calm

And look misfortune in the face

It will soon disappear

Freedom

A free spirit always

Has somewhere to go

Living without tomorrows

Wisdom

Wisdom is like the universe

Life works

Giving all

Endlessly

On Bending

If beauty in life cannot be viewed

From where you stand

Learn to bend

The Light

The light will always shine on you

Because you are so special

For every year

Celebrate

Praise it as a blessing

Ever as a Child

Become as a child again
As natural as the early sun
Rising in the morning
Retiring when the work is done